Great Inventions

THE TELEVISION

by Marc Tyler Nobleman

Consultant:
Raissa Jose Allaire
Vice President, Archives & Education
Museum of Broadcast Communications
Chicago, Illinois

Capstone
press

Mankato, Minnesota

Fact Finders is published by Capstone Press,
151 Good Counsel Drive, P.O. Box 669, Mankato, Minnesota 56002.
www.capstonepress.com

Library of Congress Cataloging-in-Publication Data
Nobleman, Marc Tyler.
    The television / by Marc Tyler Nobleman.
    p. cm.—(Fact finders. Great inventions)
    Includes bibliographical references and index.
    ISBN 0-7368-2671-8 (hardcover)
    ISBN 0-7368-4722-7 (paperback)
    1. Television—History—Juvenile literature. [1. Television—History. 2. Inventions.]
I. Title. II. Series.
TK6640.N53 2005
621.388'009—dc22   2003026412

Summary: Introduces the history and development of the television and explains how a
    television works.

Editorial Credits
Christopher Harbo, editor; Juliette Peters, series designer; Patrick Dentinger, book designer
    and illustrator; Kelly Garvin, photo researcher; Eric Kudalis, product planning editor

Photo Credits
Capstone Press/Gary Sundermeyer, 20–21, 27 (middle and right); Kelly Garvin, 1
Classic PIO Partners, cover, 18, 19, 23 (television), 26 (middle and right), 27 (left)
Corbis/Alan Towse Ecoscence, 23 (pixels); Bettmann, 5, 8, 10–11, 12, 13, 15;
    Rick Friedman, 24–25
Library of Congress, 16–17
Stock Montage Inc., 7, 9
TVHistory/Tom Genova, 26 (left)

Artistic Effects
Corel, 25 (fireworks picture); Digital Vision, 23 (scenic picture)

Table of Contents

Chapter 1

The Beatles

On the evening of February 9, 1964, millions of people turned on their televisions. They tuned into *The Ed Sullivan Show*. This weekly show had comedy acts, music acts, and dancers. That night, the show had a visiting band from England. It was the first time the Beatles played live on American TV.

The Beatles' music had already been heard in the United States. But many people had never seen the group. That night, the band played five songs.

The show set a record. About 73 million people watched the Beatles. Even today, that is a lot of people watching one TV show.

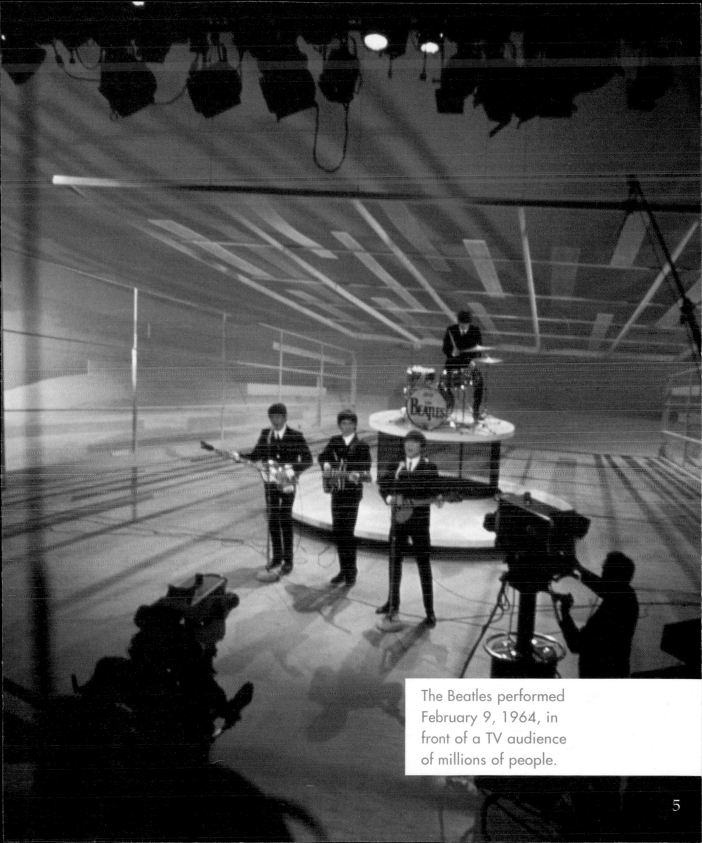

The Beatles performed February 9, 1964, in front of a TV audience of millions of people.

Chapter 2

Before Television

For thousands of years, people shared messages in simple ways. At first, people traveled between towns to share news. Later, people wrote and sent letters to each other. People carried the letters across the country by foot or on horseback.

Rise of Technology

By the late 1800s, the world was changing. People used more machines. The radio and the telephone were invented. These inventions let people send messages over long distances. By the 1920s, people could enjoy music and shows on the radio.

Before television, people listened to the radio for news and entertainment.

▲ Some early movie theaters were set up in tents. They could be moved from town to town.

In the late 1800s, movies were also invented. The moving pictures amazed people. Movies quickly became popular. Scientists looked for ways to send moving pictures over long distances.

FACT!

Samuel Morse invented the telegraph in the mid-1800s. It sent messages over wires. The messages were sent in dots and dashes called Morse code.

Mechanical Television

The mechanical television was an early idea for sending moving pictures over long distances. John Logie Baird from Scotland built a mechanical television in the 1920s. It used a spinning disk that could copy a picture line by line. Then each line could be sent to another disk. That disk would put the image back together.

John Logie Baird's mechanical television used spinning disks to make moving ▼ pictures. Baird used the head of a dummy to test his machine's pictures.

Chapter 3

Inventors of Television

Modern television was invented over many years. Philo T. Farnsworth and Vladimir Zworykin were two early inventors. Their work led to the televisions people watch today.

Philo T. Farnsworth

Philo T. Farnsworth was an American electrical engineer. When he was 14 years old, Farnsworth had an idea. He believed he could divide a picture into lines. These lines could be turned into radio **signals**. The signals could be sent from one place to another. Then the lines could be put together again to form the picture.

Philo T. Farnsworth points at the small screen of his television.

In 1927, Farnsworth put his idea
to work. He invented a **vacuum** tube
called the image dissector. It was an
early television camera. It could change
a picture into a radio signal. Farnsworth
sent the first electronic television picture.
The picture he sent was a straight line he
had painted on a piece of glass.

Farnsworth's image dissector, seen in his left hand, changed
▼ pictures into radio signals.

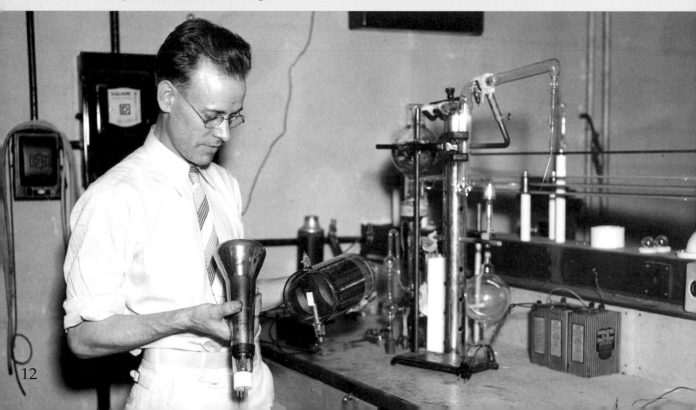

Vladimir Zworykin

Vladimir Zworykin was an electrical engineer from Russia. He moved to the United States in 1919. In 1923, Zworykin applied for a **patent** for his iconoscope. The iconoscope could also change a picture into a radio signal.

Zworykin did not get his patent for many years. Meanwhile, he struggled to make the iconoscope work. Finally, in the mid-1930s, he was able to send a picture with the iconoscope. He received a patent for the iconoscope in 1938.

▲ Vladimir Zworykin holds a vacuum tube from one of his early televisions.

FACT!

Early inventors used different names for the television. Some of these names were radiovision, radiovisor, and televisor.

While he worked on the iconoscope, Zworykin invented a picture tube in 1929. He called it the kinescope. The kinescope was an early television receiver. It was a vacuum tube that could receive radio signals. It changed the radio signals back into pictures.

Legal Problems

The invention of the television led to legal problems for Zworykin and Farnsworth. Zworykin worked for the Radio Corporation of America (RCA). RCA was not happy that Farnsworth got a patent for his invention first. The patent meant RCA had to pay Farnsworth to make and sell television vacuum tubes. After many court battles, RCA paid Farnsworth for his ideas.

Zworykin shows one of his early televisions. It used a mirror to reflect the picture from the kinescope.

Chapter 4

Television Becomes Popular

Farnsworth and Zworykin's inventions quickly became popular. By the late 1930s, people could buy the first black-and-white televisions. At the same time, the first TV stations formed.

Early Years

Many people saw TVs for the first time at the 1939 New York World's Fair. Companies like General Electric, Westinghouse Electric, and RCA showed TVs at the fair. The first TVs sold for $200 to $600.

R.C.A. COMMUNICATIONS, INC

People crowded around the TV on display at the 1939 New York World's Fair.

▲ Many TVs in the 1950s had large wood cabinets.

In 1939, the National Broadcasting Company (NBC) began TV broadcasts on the opening day of the World's Fair. That year, NBC was the first network to show a baseball game on TV. NBC also broadcast cartoons, cooking shows, and music shows.

New Features

By the 1950s, TVs had many new features. Color TVs went on sale in 1953. The first remote controls were added in the early 1950s. They were attached to the TV by a cable. The first wireless remote control came out in 1956.

FACT!

Closed captioning was invented in the 1970s. This feature prints spoken words across the screen. Closed captioning became available on TVs in the 1980s.

Changing Styles

TV styles have changed over the years. Early TVs had small screens. Their parts were tucked in large wooden frames. By the 1970s and 1980s, TVs were built with more plastic. They were made in many shapes and sizes. Today, some TVs can be held in one hand. Others have wide screens like movie screens.

The 1972 JVC Video Sphere TV had a plastic body. It was shaped to look like a space helmet. ▼

Chapter 5

How a Television Works

Broadcasting stations send out picture and sound signals. Televisions create pictures and sounds from the signals they receive. Picture signals go to the TV screen. Sound signals go to the speakers.

Cathode-Ray Tube

Most TVs use a **cathode**, an **anode**, and a screen to show pictures. These parts make up a cathode-ray tube. This sealed tube has no air.

Most of the space inside a TV is taken up by the cathode-ray tube.

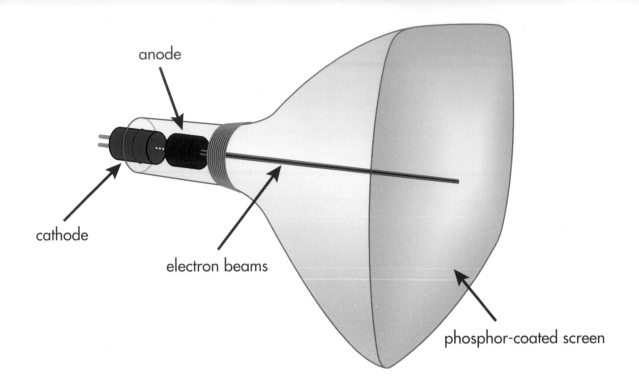

anode

cathode

electron beams

phosphor-coated screen

A cathode-ray tube uses electron beams to draw pictures on a TV screen.

A cathode is a heated wire. It releases **electrons**. An electron is one of the tiny pieces of an atom. An anode focuses the electrons into a beam. The beam of electrons is shot at the screen. The screen is coated with **phosphor**. Phosphor is a material that glows when electrons hit it. The cathode-ray tube directs electrons across the screen.

Dots and Lines

The pictures on a TV screen are made up of dots and lines. The electron beam draws each picture dot by dot, line by line. Each still picture is made up of 525 lines. The beam creates 30 still pictures each second. At this speed, the human brain sees the still pictures as moving pictures.

Blue, green, and red dots make up the pictures on a color TV.

23

Chapter 6

Television Today

The main parts of a television changed very little for 65 years. The cathode-ray tube has been used since the first black-and-white television. In recent years, companies have found new ways to create images on TV screens.

Building a Better Picture

Today, digital television is changing the shape and style of TVs. Digital television uses a **digital signal** to make pictures. Digital signals carry very clear sound and pictures. They also carry pictures that are wider than most TVs can show.

▲ HDTVs have wide screens. Some are now made thin enough to hang on a wall.

Many companies make high-definition televisions (HDTVs) to receive digital signals. HDTVs have wide screens. They give people the feeling they are watching a movie screen.

HDTVs do not use cathode-ray tubes. Instead, they use liquid crystal displays (LCDs) and plasma displays. LCDs pass light through liquid crystals to form images. Plasma displays pass an electric current through a gaslike material called plasma. The plasma shines light on phosphors to create pictures. LCD and plasma TVs create sharper pictures than TVs with cathode-ray tubes.

Televisions through the Years

Andrea 8-F-12

1939

RCA

1947

Capehart

1953

Staying Connected

Many people did not own a TV 65 years ago. Since then, TV has changed our lives. It entertains us. It delivers news. It lets people learn about each other. TV connects people around the world.

Zenith
1971

GE Spacemaker
1992

Sony Plasma TV
2003

Fast Facts

- In 1927, Philo T. Farnsworth invented the image dissector. He transmitted the first electronic television image.

- In 1929, Vladimir Zworykin invented the kinescope. The kinescope was able to receive signals and turn them into pictures.

- Most TVs use a vacuum tube called a cathode-ray tube to display images.

- On a TV screen, an electron beam creates 30 still pictures each second. At this speed, the human brain sees the still images as moving pictures.

- The National Broadcasting Company (NBC) began regular TV broadcasts from the New York World's Fair in 1939.

- The first color TVs went on sale in 1953.

- High-definition TVs (HDTVs) use liquid crystal or plasma displays to form images on a screen.

Hands On: TV News

TV news programs keep people up to date on important local and world events. Ask an adult to help you make your own TV news program for your friends.

What You Need

local newspaper   video camera
paper   desk
pencil   chair

What You Do
1. Read the latest news in a local newspaper.
2. Choose three news stories.
3. On a piece of paper, write your own reports about the stories. Try to pick out the most important information from each story.
4. Set up a video camera in front of the desk. Place the chair behind your "news" desk. Sit at your news desk. Ask an adult helper to focus the camera on you.
5. Ask your helper to begin recording. Read each story in a slow, clear voice. Look at the camera as much as possible.
6. When finished, show your news program to your friends.

What differences do you see between watching news stories and reading about them in the newspaper?

Glossary

anode (AN-ohd)—a positive electrode inside a TV that focuses electrons into a beam

cathode (KATH-ohd)—a negative electrode in a TV that releases electrons

digital signal (DIJ-uh-tuhl SIG-nuhl)—a TV signal made of a stream of numbers that can be changed into pictures and sound

electron (i-LEK-tron)—one of the tiny parts of an atom; TVs use a beam of electrons to create images on a screen.

patent (PAT-uhnt)—a legal paper that gives an inventor the right to make and sell an invention

phosphor (FAHS-for)—a material that gives off light when exposed to light or other forms of energy

signal (SIG-nuhl)—a radio, sound, or light wave that sends information from one place to another

vacuum (VAK-yoom)—a tube that has no air or other matter in it

Internet Sites

FactHound offers a safe, fun way to find Internet sites related to this book. All of the sites on FactHound have been researched by our staff.

Here's how:
1. Visit *www.facthound.com*
2. Type in this special code **0736826718** for age-appropriate sites. Or enter a search word related to this book for a more general search.
3. Click on the **Fetch It** button.

FactHound will fetch the best sites for you!

Read More

Gibson, Diane. *Television.* Making Contact. Mankato, Minn.: Smart Apple Media, 2000.

Mattern, Joanne. *Television: Window to the World.* Technology that Changed the World. New York: PowerKids Press, 2003.

Stille, Darlene R. *Television.* Let's See. Minneapolis: Compass Point Books, 2002.

Index